PRIMARY READERS
MOVERS

Pedro's Project

Aurora Martorell
Illustrator: Pedro Penizotto

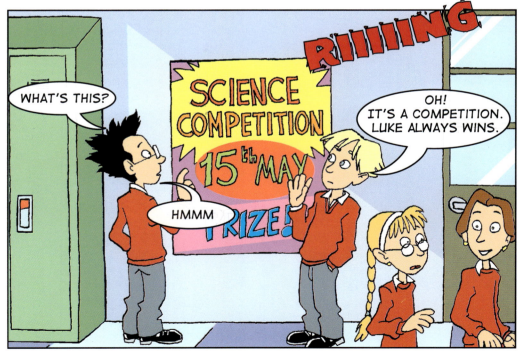

Can they open the door?

Picture Dictionary

British · cut down · danger
dining hall · experiment · football match
gardener · hide · pot
rainforest · scientist · team